BETWEEN MUSIC

LIFE IS WHAT HAPPENS WHEN THE MUSIC STOPS

Be happy

Andy G

ANDY GREENHOUSE

ISBN: 9798373960670

Words Andy Greenhouse ©2023

Sketches Andy Greenhouse ©2023

Artwork/ Cover Design Meek ©2023

Andy has asserted his moral rights

An Inherit The Earth Publication ©2023

In conjunction with Amazon

Edited by CT Meek

First published 2023

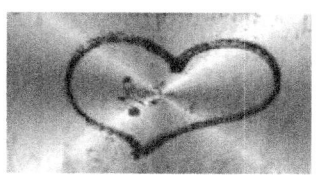

I blame it all on Terpsichore,
but I am grateful to many more.
So many names, too many to mention,
but here's a few so please pay attention -
thank you Bill Johnson, you were one of a kind,
and my mates Kev and Ben, who flicked the switch in
my mind,
to TV On The Radio and the John Peel Show,
the Old Grey Whistle Test and even TOTP, I know!
But any dedication would seem insincere,
without acknowledging those near and dear,
so this is for Wendy, my wife so sweet
for she is the music that makes my heart beat.

♪ SETLIST

- ♪ Intro
- ♪ Introspective Retrospection
- ♪ What Not To Say To Guitar Playing Demigods
- ♪ From Mama Mia To Malcolm McLaren
- ♪ Yea Though I Walk Through The Valley Of Pop I Shall Not Fear Punk
- ♪ The King Is Dead, Long Live The ... Er ... Anarchist
- ♪ The Electrifying First Orgasm Of A Concert Virgin
- ♪ 101 Things To Do And Smirk At In Brussels
- ♪ Time Travel Is Just A Tangent Off Of A Thought Process
- ♪ Guten Morgen Deutschland!
- ♪ My Sunday Girl
- ♪ Across The Crowded Disco Room
- ♪ You Wanted The Best And You Got It
- ♪ Bill, Caroline, Johnny, Rick, Francis, Alan, John And Me
- ♪ Richie? Oh Yeah! Graham Bonnet? Incredible Vocalist!
- ♪ About Fast Food, Love, Life And Death
- ♪ Hello!
- ♪ The Denim Emotive
- ♪ Outro

♪ INTRO

Many musical interludes ago, a young lad had his aural synapses twanged just as he was passing from childhood into full the blown puberty ridden angst of his teen years. What follows is the story of that transition and his journey through those formative years to emerge as a young adult with a broadly eclectic taste in music.

Discover how events during his early life are interconnected, with music as the common denominator, and how he comes to recognise the amazing coincidences that stalk him. Read how he is ripped from a sheltered infancy swaddled by the muzak of cardiganed crooners and careened through a raucous youth fuelled by the rise of rock and the power of punk. And watch as he realises how life always goes on between the music.

This is his story. My story. All the characters are real people, and this was their stage as much as mine for they all played their part. I haven't changed their names for they deserve their recognition.

♪ INTROSPECTIVE RETROSPECTION

In moments of retrospect, whether random or inspired, I often consider events from my past and try to make sense of how they form the chain reaction that has become my life. Without a doubt, the events surrounding my transition from child to teenager were the most momentous, and many memories of those halcyon days are still vividly imprinted in my mind.

This story starts in 1974 when I was twelve, although its roots delve further back through the years...

We lived in Cheltenham at the time and childhood was wonderful. It was a time of innocence, freedom and blissful ignorance. Mum and dad, me and my younger sister. We lived in the quaintly named Tommy Taylors Lane, just a stone's throw from the racecourse and the boating lake and 18 hole pitch and putt.

Dad was a career-minded soldier so it was known and accepted that our residence there would be a short lived one. It would be three years at most and we'd already been there for well over two, so feet were starting to itch. But we were seasoned travellers by then and another move on the horizon was just another beginning, more new friends and strange new territories to explore. No big deal.

Until he told us we were moving to Guildford.

To save you the trouble, this is from Wikipedia:

The Guildford pub bombings occurred on 5 October 1974. The Provisional Irish Republican Army (IRA) detonated two 6-pound gelignite bombs at two pubs in Guildford, England. The pubs were targeted because they were popular with British Army personnel. Four soldiers and one civilian were killed, whilst a further sixty-five were wounded.

And that's when I developed awareness with a capital WTF!

The bombings were obviously major news at the time, and for some time afterwards. I recall several conversations with concerned friends who had also developed awareness and realized we were moving to a place where we would probably die quite horribly, blown to smithereens, at the hands of some mad Irish maniac.

But obviously the Irish maniacs were busy elsewhere because after we arrived in Woodbridge Road, sometime in the spring of 1975, they let me enter my teenage years without any further ado.

And thus began my awakening. It would be over a year until my ears became fully attuned to the real world. A waiting period of mundane pubescence interspersed with a plethora of teenage angst and a few acutely embarrassing moments... although that is the curse of introspective retrospection... a moment from the past perceived as embarrassing in the present was quite probably perfectly innocuous way back then.

But the dice were cast, the stage was set, and strange and raucous forces were irrevocably set in motion.

My journey into musical enlightenment was under way. Bill Grundy's infamous Sex Pistols live TV interview was still over a year away, I was living in Guildford - hometown of The Stranglers; Zeppelin had just released *Physical Graffiti* and Abba were the toast of Eurovision with *'Waterloo.'*

And I bought my first ever album, called *'At The Hop'* - a compilation of 50's and 60's rock n roll songs by the likes of Bill Haley and Little Richard.

Was there any hope for me?

♪ WHAT NOT TO SAY TO GUITAR PLAYING DEMIGODS

Guildford was a bustling cathedral city, still licking its wounds and recovering from the horror of the previous October when we moved there.

Our new home had the curious address of Flat 8, The TA Centre, Woodbridge Road. There were two blocks of four flats, two up and two down, in an L shape with a small area of greenery in the centre. The four bottom flats had back gardens. Us loftier souls in the top flats, had the views. Behind our block of flats was a large car sales plot, with the busy A3 main road just beyond that. Behind the other block was an overgrown football pitch and derelict spectator stands. To the right of our little enclave, and separating us from Woodbridge Road itself was the actual TA Centre, which was no more than a few old Nissan huts and a wooden office with the nose of an aircraft protruding from one end that was used as a basic training simulator.

And to the fore was a large building site that would eventually become some new houses and a working men's club.

The glorious view from my bedroom window.

And the view from the front door.

We were evidently not in paradise.

Being so secluded from the Guildford hubbub, the only social interaction to be had apart from school was with the other residents. I was fairly lucky in that respect as there were two lads who were around the same age as me, so it was convenient to knock around with them.

All the circumstances were in conjunction, and the strange forces that were in control of my conditioning had found the on switch of my cognitive mechanism. Music began to follow me...

Perhaps one of the first inklings I had in this new existence was in the form of a letter from a friend in Cheltenham.

Simon and I were friends for the short time I'd lived there and gone to school with him. Our friendship was cruelly torn asunder when I moved to Guildford, but we kept in touch, for a short while anyway. He even came to visit once, but it wasn't the same and the pen-pal friendship soon fizzled out.

But I digress.

In one of his letters to me he mentioned strange unheard-of things. He spoke of his record collection, albeit a small one, and the ones he intended to buy soon. He spoke of Queen. *A Night At The Opera. Sheer Heart Attack.* I was totally bemused and ignorant as I didn't have a clue what he was on about. I was still under parental influence. Nana Mouskouri, Demis Roussos, Cliff Richard, Sound of Music, South Pacific to name a few of the groovy sounds that my ears had suffered throughout my childhood. As mentioned previously, my first conscious record buying decision resulted in my ownership of a 50's and 60's Rock and Roll compilation album.

I was primed and ready.

Using my skills of introspective retrospection, I have identified a defining moment from this period in the wilderness. My friend Cliff who lived in Flat 2, which was diagonally opposite ours, had an older sister. I don't remember seeing her around very much but on this one occasion she was at home, with her boyfriend. And he had a guitar! I was quite awestruck. This was only my second close-up encounter with a guitar playing demigod and here I was in his presence while he played. Don't ask me what he actually played up until the point he spoke to me as I really don't recall. All I know is he was really good and for all I know he went on to become Rick Parfitt or Brian May because I never saw him again. Although come to think of it, Mr. Parfitt did wave at me a few years later, but that's another story.

When the maestro finished strumming, he had to push back his long hair which had fallen over his face whilst playing. That done he looked over at me and asked me the sixty-four-million-dollar question, *"What do you want me to play?"*

Me! He was asking me! Me, whose comfort zone included people with unpronounceable names in large dresses, and whimsical costumed actors that sang instead of speaking. In desperation I hedged my bets and plumped for the most popular thing I knew at the time. It had to be popular; he had to know it because the whole of Europe loved them.

I uttered the words that will haunt me till my dying day, *"Do you know any Abba?"*

He laughed and laughed. Any hope I might have had was fading fast.

♪ FROM MAMA MIA TO MALCOLM MCLAREN

The long dry summer of '75 passed in a blur.

Exploration of new surroundings and anticipation of a new school in the September were the main culprits. The favourite place for just plain messing about was behind the other flats to ours. There was an old football pitch with some tiered spectator stands and even an old wooden structure that used to be some sort of covered seating, but the whole place was derelict and totally overgrown with weeds and huge clumps of bushes. It was a great adventure ground for kids.

Sometimes I would amble into Guildford town centre, just to have a look around, although this meant walking the entire length of Woodbridge Road, which seemed endless. There was an upside to this epic trek though, if only out of morbid curiosity. I had found a hobby model shop selling Airfix kits in Swan Lane, which was a narrow alley way that joined the parallel roads of the High Street and North Street. The shop was also just a few yards further down from The Seven Stars public house, which had been the second target of the Irish maniacs the previous autumn. I felt strange being so close to a place associated with such horror.

School was altogether more daunting. In Cheltenham I'd passed my 11+ exams and had just finished two years at the Grammar School there. On moving to Guildford, I learnt that I would be going to the Woking County Grammar School for Boys, which was only about 5 or 6 miles away and took around half an hour on the public transport bus I had to catch. It never even crossed my mind why I wasn't attending the Grammar School in Guildford. Acceptance of situations was a part of my life and so off I trudged every morning, to the bus stop at the far end of Stockton Road. Another seemingly endless walk.

I was placed in form 3M, the M denoting 'Magnanimously' from the school motto of 'Justly, Skilfully, Magnanimously.' The Headmaster was obviously very astute at character determination when he put me in that particular form. It was a fairly strict school, steeped in tradition and history.

The teachers were all male, mostly elderly, usually wearing the trademark flowing gowns over their tweed or corduroy suits with patched elbows, and always addressed as Sir.

As educations go, mine was a fairly enjoyable one. I spent the rest of 1975 settling in and finding my feet in my new environment and soon started making some friends. And all the time music was inveigling its way into my life, from a multitude of sources, teasing my aural synapses with veiled hints of harmonies the future held in store.

Confusion that Christmas saw my sister and I both receiving a single from the parents. Single, as in a flat round piece of vinyl, usually black, seven inches across, which when played at 45rpm on a record player produced music of some sort. Except the one I unwrapped was *'Hold Me Close'* by David Essex, and hers was Slade's perennial *'Merry Christmas Everybody.'* I think it was maybe the look on our faces that prompted dad to sheepishly admit his tagging error.

The actual Number 1 in the charts at Christmas was Queens all time classic, *'Bohemian Rhapsody.'* But even that was not enough to convince me of their ability and worthiness, besides I really didn't understand what they were on about. I was still clinging to the last vestiges of my comfort zone and saw in the birth of the year that would prove to be the turning point in my musical life, bopping away to *'Mama Mia'* as ABBA enjoyed a resurgence in their popularity with the New Year's Number 1.

And so began 1976, with a bunch of clean-cut Swedish warblers, and steadily regressed from there. I revelled in such delights as Slik's *'Forever and Ever',* The Brotherhood of Man's Eurovision success of *'Save Your Kisses For Me'* and more ABBA with *'Fernando'* and *'Dancing Queen'.* And if that wasn't enough to turn an impressionable young lad into an anorak wearing nerd, I also had to endure the melodically challenged Telly Savalas talking through *'If'* and suffer the Ooh-Arrr'ness of The Wurzels *'Combine Harvester'.* My descent into pop purgatory was almost complete.

The final straw came out of an act of impulsive desperation and was almost as embarrassing as my encounter with the guitar demigod.

There was to be an auction at School during one of the lunch breaks, run by some older boys to raise funds. The room was packed when I got there but I managed to squeeze my way to the front just in time. The next Lot was a bag of 4 LP's which would be ideal to start off my meagre record collection. Surprisingly nobody bid for them, so I started it off with the ridiculously low bid of 5 pence. I almost won it there and then until the eagle-eyed auctioneer spotted another bidder at the back of the room who must have been signalling his bids because I never heard him. The price kept going up, but I eventually wore the other bidder down and I won for the bargain price of 75 pence! I quickly paid up and clutching my prized new possessions protectively to my chest, I squeezed back out of the crowd, very pleased with myself. I was now the proud owner of four of K-Tel's finest pressings! The exact albums escape me, but after browsing their website for reminders, titles such as *'20 Dynamic Hits of the 70s, 22 Greatest No. 1 singles* or *'Christmas Disco Party Hits'* ring a few alarm bells.

I was in as deep as I was going to get and my only hope was Malcolm McLaren.

♪ YEA THO I WALK THRU THE VALLEY OF POP I SHALL FEAR NOT PUNK

Unbeknown to me, momentous things were afoot during the early parts of '76 that carried on through the sweltering summer months.

I do remember it being very hot around that time, but according to Wikipedia it was actually the hottest summer in the UK since records began, with temperatures well into the eighties for most of June and July and, for 15 consecutive days it was over ninety degrees F. Hot!

And as England cooked, a new breed of music which had been simmering since early in the year reached a boiling point and exploded on an unsuspecting public.

Under the management of my saviour, Mr. Malcolm McLaren, The Sex Pistols began their rise to notoriety with a series of gigs that usually ended in a fracas of mayhem, violence and destruction.

Their first major gig was as support act to Eddie and

the Hot Rods, which ended in the aforementioned chaos. The journalistic review of this gig was the inspiration behind the formation of another band, The Buzzcocks, by two guys who travelled from Bolton to track the Pistols down.

The Sex Pistols built up a hardcore following, including such names as Billy Idol, Siouxsie Sioux and Steve Severin or, as they were dubbed, the Bromley Contingent. They began touring bigger venues such as the Marquee and the Nashville but were soon banned from both of these.

Early July saw them headlining gigs supported by the newly formed Clash and the Damned. Joe Strummer of the Clash had been the singer in a band at one of their earlier pub venues and seen something prophetic in their performance. He saw the coming of punk, in the guise of the Sex Pistols. On July 20th they performed their anthem tune for the first time, *'Anarchy In The UK.'*

Meanwhile, back in the zone, I was happily engrossed in the cuteness of Kiki Dee duetting with Elton John as they knocked Demis Roussos off the number 1 spot with *'Don't Go Breaking My Heart.'*

I was still in pop purgatory.

But on the bright side, possibly inspired by Ms. Dee, I had started to notice the attraction that girls had. Well, one in particular... another denizen of the TA flats and younger sister of one of my two friends. She went by the name of Fiona and she had ginger hair. The relationship was sweet but never got past the holding hands stage. I think what killed it was when I learnt she did a paper round at stupid o'clock every morning and expected me to accompany her. I managed it once and that was enough.

The heatwave and long drought finally broke in the September, just in time for the return to school. ABBA's *'Dancing Queen'* gyrated its way up the charts as the rain fell and fell, and the Sex Pistols began a tour of Britain.

In October it still rained.

Pussycat toppled ABBA with *'Mississippi'* and on the 8th, EMI signed the Pistols to a two year contract. *'Anarchy In The UK'* was released as a single in late November, not long after Chicago's impassioned blackmail of *'If You Leave Me Now'* chased Pussycat off the top spot.

December 1st and one of the most defining moments in British TV, and music's, history was witnessed by many outraged viewers.

The Sex Pistols, and some of the Bromley Contingent, were invited to appear on the live TV evening show 'Today' on Thames TV, hosted by Bill Grundy.

Goaded by the host who claimed to be drunk, and after a somewhat lewd exchange with Siouxsie Sioux, the guests were encouraged to say something outrageous. The words sod, bastard, fucker and fucking were said in consecutive sentences by Steve Jones. On live TV. The Upright Public were apoplectic and next morning, the whole school was buzzing with it. I was suitably shocked and impressed in all the right places when hearing it being retold numerous times by those that had actually watched it.

My days in purgatory were numbered.

Punk wasn't born. It was ripped, screaming, cursing and puking from the hearts of disillusioned youth and it was going to be my lifeline.

♪ YOLO POGO

I once tried

to pogo

after four pints

of lager and half

a dozen No. 6

I coughed

me guts up

fucked

me knees up

and the beer

ended up

thrown up

down the back

of the bloke

in front

now forty years

later

don't smoke

hardly drink

and me knees

are still

fucked

but get me

to the gig

and it's

go buddy go

and the bloke

in front

still thinks

I'm a cunt

yolo

pogo.

♪ THE KING IS DEAD! LONG LIVE THE... ER... ANARCHIST!

1977.

My last year in pop purgatory.

Like a condemned man about to be cast out from the society that had nurtured and protected him, I was allowed a few last months to cherish all that I was giving up and leaving behind. So, I got into what all red-blooded young lads of my age did - I became a fan of the Rock Follies on TV.

This was a comedy musical drama about three girls in a band called 'Little Ladies' and all about their trials and tribulations as they tried to make it big in the music world.

Perhaps one of the most ironic things about this situation was the cast, in particular the character Anna Wynd. This was played by Charlotte Cornwell. A surname shared with the lead singer of the Stranglers, namely Hugh Cornwell, who would also figure greatly in my life of musical appreciation.

Julie Covington, another of the lead actresses, released a single from the show, the very powerful *'Don't Cry For Me Argentina'* and later turned down the role in the stage show that featured that song, Evita.

The year produced some of the best music I would eventually listen to, but I was oblivious to this as I sucked up such dross as David Soul's *'Don't Give Up On Us,'* The Floaters asking us to *'Float On'* with them, more ABBA and even the Brotherhood of Man bouncing back for more after their previous years victory in Eurovision with a new hit, *'Angelo.'*

We even had a touch of country from Kenny Rogers getting on his knees for *'Lucille.'* 'Baccara told us *Yes Sir, I Can Boogie,'* the Jacksons wanted to *'Show You The Way To Go,'* and the year culminated in the awesomely gruesome *'Mull of Kintyre'* from Paul McCartney's Wings.

While all of this was going on, other forces were at work, trying to attract my attention.

My sister introduced a boyfriend who was somewhat older than her, and me for that matter. Soon I was listening to Genesis, but only when he visited, and to this day I still prefer their older stuff. The only two albums I recall him bringing and playing were *'Nursery Cryme'* and *'The Lamb Lies Down on Broadway'*, which was the last to feature Peter Gabriel which may also explain my preference for their older work.

Somewhere along the way I attended a party/disco to which a whole load of lads from school went. Two things stick in my mind from that night. The first was 'doing the cave' being the dance motion one makes in time to music by Status Quo... hands on hips, bend down to the left twice, straighten up and swing shoulders twice then bend down to the right twice, straighten up and repeat ad infinitum. The mighty Quo did not unfortunately make a musical impact on me that night. That would come soon. It was just the incredibly energetic dancing that engaged me.

The other moment from that night was *'Brown Sugar.'* My first introduction to the Rolling Stones, and the only thing of theirs I have ever liked. I have never bought a single Stones record, and never will. I just never somehow connected with them, but *'Brown Sugar'* was just ... loud and brilliant. You can't please all the people all the time, eh?

It was about this time that I also discovered the joys of classical music. Well, not ALL classical music obviously, but from that time three remain firmly entrenched in my mind as 'must have' music. Tchaikovsky's *1812 Overture,* Elgar's Pomp and Circumstance March *No.1 Land of Hope and Glory* and Strauss's *Also Sprach Zarathustra.* I could play all these just as loud as my most raucous punk or metal and enjoy them for their rousing qualities just as much.

Over the years I have added such delights as Holst's *Planet Suite,* Khachaturian's *Sabre Dance* and Verdi's *Four Seasons.* There are others no doubt, but none will move me the same way as these have done.

To top it all, punk music finally got a grip of bored teenagers everywhere. Although beaten to the release by the Buzzcocks, the Clash and the Damned, in mid-April the Stranglers, fronted by the aforementioned Hugh Cornwell, released *Rattus Norvegicus*, an act that although significant to the extreme passed me by until friends started talking about it. The song *'Peaches'* in particular. Apparently, it was so lewd that it was banned by the BBC and an edited version had to be made before it was aired.

I was desperate to hear it.

Of course, what made the Stranglers even more popular, for us at any rate, was the fact they came from Guildford. I could have rubbed shoulders with them in the street, not that I would have known. But we felt kind of special to be associated with them, albeit in such a small insignificant way. It wasn't until years later that I learnt they were only based there, not actually from there.

It just so happened that the drummer, Jet Black, ran an off-licence which the band used as a base in their early days.

But what all this boiled down to was that I was being bombarded with music, of all genres and styles, from all directions. Without realizing it, I was becoming the most musically eclectic teenager on the planet, and I was in dire need of definition, identity and direction!

Perhaps the catalyst came in the summer. On August 16th Elvis Presley was found dead at his home, Graceland in Memphis. To say it was the end of an era would be an understatement, but the king of rock 'n roll was dead, and the world of music was going to change irrevocably forever. I remember hearing the news but not feeling anything particularly emotional.

The penny finally dropped for me in September. I'd turned 15 in the June and was now in the 5th form, 5M, at Woking Grammar. I had also started a Saturday job working in a bookshop in Guildford town centre for which

I was paid the princely sum of £5 for a day's work, but to add injury to insult I was paid monthly into a bank account! Still, it helped me buy a fair few records in the following months.

On September 23rd the Stranglers released their second studio album, *No More Heroes*. I was captivated the minute I heard the opening riff of the title track and by the end of the month I'd been to Woolworth's and coughed up the two and half quid and bought my first real record. Hugh, JJ, Dave and Jet were the posse that pulled me from the depths of pop purgatory although I was going to have to wait until the following May for their next album.

My outlook on life and music changed dramatically. I began buying the weekly music newspaper Sounds, a paper I much preferred over the more established *NME (New Musical Express)* and I started feeling the urge to rebel against the conformist life I had been brought up in.

I wasn't a very convincing rebel though... I think I was about 42 when I finally got a Mohican, and there was no way I was going to get away with wearing plastic bin liners, chains, ripped t-shirts and safety pins through various parts of my anatomy!

I recall visibly wincing while watching a friend having his ear pierced with a safety pin, by his girlfriend at the youth club one Friday night. Hmm ... no thank you!

And so punk music woke me up to what lay beyond pop. It wasn't to become a way of life but it gave a meaning and direction. I whiled away the rest of the year listening to and buying albums by such greats as Eddie And The Hot Rods *Life On The Line*, Ian Dury *New Boots And Panties*, and the self-titled The Boomtown Rats to name a few.

Highlight of the late year releases was of course the Sex Pistols, under their latest and final label signing of Virgin, with their absolutely legendary *Never Mind The Bollocks*.

After that, for me, punk was dead. It evolved. It had to because it could not surpass an album like that. It was the ultimate in crass and I began to seek new satisfaction and found it in many places, as a new wave of punk rolled in, and also as I began to realise there was other musical talent out there that was tickling my ears. My appreciation really started to diversify.

1978 was going to be a loud year.

♪ THE ELECTRIFYING FIRST ORGASM OF A CONCERT VIRGIN

By the time May of 1978 came around, punk was old hat. I had witnessed day zero and would live to tell my grandchildren about that wondrous time, but it was becoming repetitive.

A new wave of bandwagoneers was already emerging and the sound was very samey.

The Stranglers released their third album, *Black and White* which proved to be the pinnacle of my interest in punk music because of one song.

When the album was first released the original marketing plan was to press the first few thousand copies in black vinyl for the A side and white for the B, but that was going to prove too costly and difficult so instead the album was produced as a normal black pressing, but as an added extra freebie in the first 70 thousand or so copies there was included a 7" single in white vinyl. On the A side of this little gem was their cover of a Dionne Warwick song written by Bacharach and David, *'Walk On*

By.' I still play this track today. It is probably the best song the Stranglers ever recorded and therefore, would not be bettered.

By the time it was released I was already listening to lots of other music that I hadn't experienced before and hearing *'Walk On By'* merely confirmed my suspicions.

Punk was dead, so death to all but metal!

Yes, I had seen the light. Jesus H tap-dancing Christ, I had seen the light and it was my mate Paul, who everyone called Ben, that flicked the switch.

I think our friendship started on the bus to school every day. He wasn't in my form at school. I believe he was of the J (for Justly) variety, so I didn't actually have much interaction with him there, but on the half hour or so ride between home and school there was time, and we soon became good friends. One of the pastimes we used to engage in on the bus trips was scrabbling around on the floor under the seats looking for dog-ends of discarded cigarettes. When we had enough, we would break them apart to get at the remnants of the tobacco and then roll one of our own. They would taste absolutely foul, but it saved having to buy them.

With my birthday being in June I was one of the youngest in my year at school and as a result could only look on in great envy as several of my friends acquired mopeds as soon as they turned 16. I was always the kid that had to plead to have a go at sitting on it and revving the throttle if I was lucky.

The most popular bike by far was the Yamaha FS-1E, commonly called the 'Fizzy'. By the time I turned 16 my days in England would be numbered and it would be pointless in buying one. Consequently, I would miss out on a very important foundation for the culture that I would eventually end up immersing myself in.

Ben/Paul was no exception, except he did things differently. He had a bike, but it wasn't a fizzy, being more of a hybrid mix of moto-cross and road, with his own paintjob. He also had sideburns too of which I was intensely envious, not that I would ever let on. Something else that made him exceptionally cool in my eyes was that he owned a computer game! Now, bear in mind we're talking about 1978 here so when I say computer game what I'm actually referring to is one of the very first consoles that were made by Binatone. You know the one, where a square ball bounces around the screen and you have to manoeuvre your paddle up and down your side of the screen in order to hit the ball back across the screen to your opponent's side. If you missed it and the ball disappeared off the edge, then you lost a point. There were lots of variations that could be played, all as mind-numbingly monotonous as each other. And this was all in glorious monochrome too.

But the best thing about going to Ben's to hang out, was the music he introduced me to.

In January 1969, when I was only 6 and a half, Messrs. Page, Plant, Jones and Bonham released their self-titled debut album, and a legend was created.

It took me another 9 years before I would eventually listen to the album in its entirety and that christening was one of many epiphanies I have experienced.

The first track itself *'Good Times, Bad Times'* was to become synonymous with my whole life and the band went on to become a mainstay in my musical evolvement.
I am of course talking about Led Zeppelin and their first album *Led Zeppelin.*

Ben had most of their albums, certainly the first four, which will always be their masterpiece set for me, and these were the ones we played over and over. Their second album, titled just *II* opened with the ageless classic, *'Whole Lotta Love'* which had also been in long term use as the opening theme tune to Top Of The Pops on TV, so it was a tune I was already familiar with.

But perhaps the most famous of their songs was track four of the fourth album, strangely enough entitled IV. I was drinking a glass of cheap cider and smoking a rollie in Ben's bedroom when I heard *'Stairway To Heaven'* for the first time ever. Punk might have woken me up, but it was rock that stuck its fingers in my nostrils and dragged me headfirst from my bed.

Other bands soon followed. There were just too many to listen to, but I did what I could to cross them off the list. Black Sabbath, Deep Purple, ACDC, Alice Cooper, Ted Nugent, Thin Lizzy and Judas Priest to name but a few, were soon bands that I avidly listened to at any given opportunity. Which, when you put it all together, made the band for my very first gig, a somewhat baffling choice ...

Some things get hazy over time; others will remain firmly entrenched in memory. My first ever concert is a bit of both. I shall certainly never forget the actual gig, but the events that led up to it are the hazy bits. There were a bunch of us going, five or six I believe, but I can't recall who organized it or who bought the tickets, or even who suggested it. I don't remember where we got the tickets or how much they were, although thinking about it I have the ticket stub somewhere so that will tell me some of what I've forgotten.

But in June of 1978, a few days before my 16th birthday we got on a train at Woking station and headed off to Wembley Arena to see The Electric Light Orchestra, still going strong on their *Out Of The Blue* world tour that had kicked off a few months earlier.

The atmosphere was incredible and, dare I say it, electric. The laser lighting effects were truly astounding and the music riveting. It wasn't Zep or Sabbath, but it was still rock and a whole lifetime away from the poptastic crap I had been listening to in purgatory. I was converted, not only to ELO who would go on to play a major role in the following years, but also to live music. The experience was life changing.

Two other things happened around that time that would also change my life.

The first was when I sat my GCE 'O' Level exams at school. I took eight subjects and passed four of them with 'B' grades.

The other was in July. We packed our bags and belongings once again, and left England's green and pleasant lands behind us as we set off for yet more pastures new.

We were moving to Brussels, for a short two month stay with relatives there, before heading to our ultimate destination in Germany.

I wished I'd paid more attention in my German classes.

♪♪ 101 THINGS TO DO AND SMIRK AT IN BRUSSELS

Brussels was a beautiful city.

We arrived at the right time of year to enjoy a glorious Belgian summer, in the early July of 1978.

As welcome guests of my Aunt Lynda and Uncle Richard we moved into their top floor apartment in the Avenue des Coccinelles, located in the Watermael-Boitsfort suburb of the city. This was to be our home for the next two months before we could head out to Germany once military accommodation was available there. Dad had to leave us in Brussels as he had already started his new posting, so with nothing to do but just enjoy life we got on with living it.

The apartment block was only a very short walk away from the nearest tram stop. For the purchase of a single ticket, you could travel all day, on and off the trams as many times as you liked, so trips into the city centre were always looked forward to. My sister and I often went on our own, but the most enjoyable ones were when we were accompanied by Lynda and Richard who knew their way around and were also fun to be with.

We did the whole tourist thing with them. The Grand Place, (pronounced Plass), the Atomium, (big silver balls on tubes), Waterloo, (no, NOT more bloody ABBA but the memorial site of the actual battle) and of course, the Mannequin Pis, (bronze statue of small boy having a pee). I was also introduced to Stella Artois before it became a fashionable drink in the UK, a few years later and I sampled snails for the first time, served in a dish of spicy sauce, which I found very tasty and have eaten them again since.

We were also introduced to two renowned Belgian delicacies, although not at the same time. The first was *'frites with mayo'*, which is basically a bag of chips (English version, not American), but cooked in such a way the taste is just amazing, especially when topped with a good dollop of mayonnaise. The second specialty was waffles. I spoiled many a shirt with the drooling just from thinking about their sweetness and taste.

But for a sixteen-year-old, the highlight of each tram ride into the city was when we stopped at a particular station. Richard alerted me to it as we approached for the first time, he obviously being well aware. As we pulled into the station, a disembodied voice would announce over the intercom the name of the station, *Kunst-Wet*. It never failed to raise a snigger or a guffaw, and if you don't know why, well sorry but you will have to remain in the dark as decorum prohibits me from explaining, without smirking again.

Two months in a foreign city had its ups and downs. It was obviously not really financially feasible to go out every single day, so we spent a fair amount of time back in the apartment as well. Being top floor, although only three stories high, there was quite a good view of the surrounding area, which was mainly housing. Set further back in the distance were some impressive high-rise blocks of flats, many floors higher than our little abode and I would spend hours peering at them through Richard's binoculars after he assured me he had once seen a woman topless sunbathing on one of the high up balconies. I never did see her.

There was a TV in the apartment, but I'm sure you can imagine how riveting programs, in French and Flemish, in 1978 were. Yes, you got it...not very! There was, however, an interesting interlude one weekend when we invented the world's first ever TV remote control device. It was essentially two bamboo sticks tied together with a pencil eraser attached to one end. In those days when the TV channels were changed by pressing a button on the front fascia this innovative device worked incredibly well, and had we patented it we could possibly have been millionaires by now. Unfortunately, it slipped down the back of the sofa and is probably still there to this day. Forgotten and fluffy.

Which just left the record player. The only problem being that all my records were packed in an MDF packing crate, in transit somewhere between Guildford and our future home in Germany. But I was in luck. Lynda and Richard had the semblance of a record collection and I managed to scrimp some of my earnings together to buy one of my own...

For some strange reason, Brussels seemed bereft of record boutiques. I'm sure that in this modern age you could probably walk down the main shopping street and come across the Belgian equivalent of HMV or Virgin Megastore, but in 1978 you just couldn't. With hindsight perhaps I missed out on another millionaire-making opportunity, but forward thinking has always been one of my shortfalls. I did however eventually stumble across some sort of musically aware shop in the murky corner of a dark alleyway. Amongst the racks of musty records by obscure foreign artists and long forgotten crooners was the object of my desire. A bell rang in my head. Visions of swaying bodies and flying hair sprang to mind as I recalled the energetic dancing at the disco a few months earlier. The record was there, waiting for me, and I had to buy it.

The album I bought was strangely prophetic in itself. It was the fourth studio album by Status Quo, named *Dog Of Two Head*. The front cover featured a picture of a dog, a British Bulldog no less, with two heads. It didn't actually feature the song we had danced 'the cave' to, but track one, side one, was a song called *Umleitung* which is German for 'diversion'. The Bulldog connotation was obviously symbolic of me, especially having two heads as I am a Gemini. And Brussels was indeed a diversion off our route to Germany. It was an album I connected with immediately and I played it to death back at the flat. It was also the record that started my lifelong adoration of the Mighty Quo. But more of that later.

From my lovely Aunt and Uncles small and insignificant record collection were just two that were totally significant at the time and for many years after. They were both albums I had never heard before. Although I had listened to Deep Purple to some extent, their *Stormbringer* was new to me, and I found this album to be exhilarating.

Probably what drew me to it was the connection of the title with a series of science fantasy books I had read by the very prolific author, Michael Moorcock. In one series the main character, Elric of Melniboné, wielded an enchanted sword with the same name. Other musical influences would become apparent in the following years that could also be attributed to Michael Moorcock, or at the very least, have a connection with him.

The other of their albums that gave me enjoyment through my Belgian diversion was Mike Oldfield's *Tubular Bells*. The range of instruments played on the album was incredible and the composition and actual sound was, I thought, fantastic. As an aside, there is much I was unaware of concerning this album right up until this very moment of writing. I was always of the impression that the voiceover reeling off the list of instruments was Mr. Oldfield himself. It turns out this was actually a chap called Vivian Stanshaw who was given the credit of 'Master of Ceremonies' on that album.

He was also known for a lot of similar work with the oddly named Bonzo Dog Doo-Dah Band. I was also unaware that Tubular Bells was the first album released by Richard Branson's Virgin Records and that he (Branson) later named two of his aircraft *Tubular Belle*. But enough of this Umleitung.

Brussels was an enjoyable time. I came away from it enriched in both cosmopolitan and musical terms.

I was ready in mind and body and soul for all that Germany could throw at me.

♪ TIME TRAVEL IS JUST A TANGENT OFF OF A THOUGHT PROCESS

Before I go any further, I feel I need to take you with me on a brief tangent of a journey, back through the hazy mists of time, to a place of childhood innocence where nothing mattered.

Come with me, back to Belgium again, to the summer of 1971.

We moved to a small town called Herentals, not far from Antwerp. This was dads latest posting and although it was only to last just over a year, I have many vivid memories from this time even though I was only nine or ten. This one concerns the inception of cognitive awareness of all things musical.

Such was the military way that when you moved somewhere you very likely knew somebody that was already there. The army moved its people around in a finite world so meeting up with people you had previously met was bound to happen often. That's how it was for dad anyway. He was still working his way up through the ranks, but he had made a lot of friends and acquaintances on the way and on arriving in Belgium it soon became apparent that he wasn't a stranger here. It turned out that the wife of one of dad's old squaddie buddies was the Akela of the local Cub Scout pack for us army kids, and it just so happened that their summer camping trip was just about to set off. Without so much as a by your leave, I was sent off to camp with a load of kids I'd never met before.

Once we arrived, it wasn't so bad. It turned out we weren't actually camping out under canvas. We were in what seemed like a huge old chateau type building and most of us boys were in a large dormitory bedroom. It was a very loud and chaotic experience, but we soon settled into a routine for the few days we were there. The chateau was set deep in a forest, somewhere in the Belgian outback. I really do not have a clue where we were, but it was great fun. We were right at the edge of a large lake in the middle of this forest. We used to run through the trees and around the shore of the lake just shouting stupid stuff for which we would be admonished by Akela. One day as we ran around, we came across a dead frog. Not dead as in died, but dead as in killed. It had been skewered to the ground with a sharp twig and we were perplexed as to who could have done it, or even why. Perhaps this trip was meant to be more intuitive than I ever imagined.

It turned out we were not alone in the forest. The whole area was actually crawling with boys from various scouting organizations that had come from far and wide for a Jamboree. But we just carried on running around the lake and shouting stupid stuff, although a little quieter than before. Then one day, toward the end of the week, I had my first ever meeting with a guitar playing demigod.

Running through the trees, unable to see what was ahead, we almost ran into someone. He was sitting cross legged, back against a tree trunk, and he was playing a guitar. I remember him vividly, short blond hair, thin face with high cheekbones but most noticeably he had deformed fingers on one hand where his index and middle fingers were fused together. But he was playing guitar, and very well too. It was just such a random occurrence and totally unexpected. He was probably about 15 or 16 and obviously with one of the scout groups but playing there in the forest he was alone. I think we engaged in some small talk whilst he strummed some more sounds from his strings, but we soon tired of it and were off again. I didn't see him again that week.

Indeed, I wouldn't see him again for a good few years.

♪ GUTEN MORGEN DEUTSCHLAND!

When I was seven, I was living in Cyprus.

Amongst the many memories I still have from that time are the trips we used to go on in dads old Morris Traveller car, all around the Cyprus countryside.

And of those trips, the thing that springs to mind most was the singing. Whether or not the car had a radio I really can't recall, although I doubt there would have been much worth listening to, considering our location.

So, on the long trips, the four of us used to sing such delights as *'She'll Be Coming Round The Mountain'* and *'In The Stores.'* If we got really desperate, we would occasionally burst into *'Ging Gang Gooley Gooley'* or the one who's title eludes me but ends something like *'..catsanella bogen by the sea.'* But we enjoyed it, and it kept us occupied, because let's face it, bored kids on a long car journey is just asking for trouble.

Fast forward about ten years:

The distance from Brussels, Belgium to Dülmen, Germany was about 150 miles and probably took us around three to four hours, in a FIAT 124 of all things.

Perhaps there was no radio and perhaps we were the English 'von Trapps', singing our way across Europe. I prefer to think I sat moodily on the back seat, studying the passing scenery in quiet contemplation of my imminent new life. Perhaps we did sing and I have mentally blocked it for I have no recollection whatsoever of that journey except for our arrival at our new home in Dülmen. Or perhaps I'm suffering from post-traumatic stress because the reason I remember our arrival so well is that on exiting the car I reached back through the open door to retrieve my jacket at the precise moment my sister decided to close the door, with my arm still inside. My first words uttered on German soil were raw Anglo-Saxon.

We had arrived in *'am Osthoff Strasse.'*, which was the name of the street.

It was the main area of military accommodation for English families in Dülmen. Running almost the length of the street down the left-hand side was a continuous terrace of houses, staggered into rows of three. About halfway down was ours, No. 12.

On the other side of the road, going off at right angles were four more terraced rows of five blocks of two houses each, making a total of about fifty houses for the families of the NCOs (Non-Commissioned Officers).

At the far end of the street were some of the Officer's houses, comprising another six abodes.

A short walk through a recreational area of kids swings and slides took you to an area of apartment blocks where there was probably somewhere in the region of another one fifty to two hundred housing units.

What this all boiled down to, was an enclave mentality. This is where we had to live, like it or not. All English, piled in next door to each other and surrounded by

Germans and all things German. There was no class or cultural differences, no north-south divide and there was certainly no pressure to conform to one particular ideal, whether it be sport, music or politically orientated.

We were all there due to forces beyond our control where everyone knew almost everyone else, and we were accepted regardless.

At the entrance to *am Osthoff*, facing down the street, was the NAAFI (Navy Army Air Force Institution). This marvellous establishment was basically a supermarket that sold a little of everything from daily groceries, electrical goods, alcohol and cigarettes (both of which you needed a ration card to buy) and, most importantly, it sold records. Within the first two weeks of our arrival, I had visited the NAAFI and, flying the flag of eclecticism at full mast, bought Blondie's *Parallel Lines* and Black Sabbath's *Never Say Die,* both of which were new releases that month. Into the basket also went the eternal *Bat Out Of Hell* by Meatloaf, which had been released almost a year earlier but was still riding the charts.

When I bought those albums, I think maybe I was sending out signals. Here I was, the new kid in town but hey, I'm into good music so I'm cool. Maybe that was the subliminal message anyway, but the albums were awesome. Parallel Lines was Blondie's second album, featuring such classics as *'Heart Of Glass'* and *'Hanging On The Telephone'* and represented my lingering affinity with the punk generation. Blondie weren't really punk, but they rose to fame riding high on the new wave of punk-inspired groups, helped along in their popularity amongst the male teen demographic in no small way by the presence of the gorgeous wet-dreaminess of Debbie Harry.

The same, however, could not be said about Marvin Lee Aday, or Meatloaf as he was better known, but boy could he sing! The album did not fit into any particular genre. It was just what it was, but it was one of the most popular records ever. In the UK alone it stayed in the charts for a massive 474 consecutive weeks (a feat only surpassed by Fleetwood Mac's *Rumours* with 478) and (at the time of writing) still sells over 200,000 copies a year today. The absolute energy and power generated by his singing was almost hypnotic and the lyrics just had to be learned and sung along to whenever the record was played.

And lastly, the Sabbath album. Their eighth, but my first, and the last to feature Ozzy Osbourne.

Ozzy actually quit the band before it was produced but returned after some of the tracks had been written with, coincidentally, Dave Walker of Fleetwood Mac fame, but he refused to do those songs until they were rewritten. But *Never Say Die* was, I felt, the death knell for Sabbath. Once an original member leaves a band, it is never really the same again, especially when it's the singer. And that's how it was with Sabbath. I never bought another record of theirs after that one but have often added one of their earlier ones to my collection as and when the opportunity to buy one arose. The album did however accelerate my appreciation of all things metal.

There were two major occurrences that started within those two weeks of arrival too.

The first was school. As previously mentioned, I had sat my GCE 'O' Levels back in the 5th form at Woking, but I had only passed four of the eight I sat, namely English Literature and Language, History and Geography. I failed French, Art, German and Maths. I had to go back to school to resit them, if only just for the Maths. But I decided to retake Art and German as well. And so, I became a 6th former. The elite. The pinnacle of classroom status. And the subject of a future chapter.

The other was Friday nights, which we soon learned, were the nights when all available youths between the ages of 12 and 18 were rounded up and herded aboard an army issue bus and then transported onto the base, to attend the weekly Youth Club. And the mainstay of any YC night, as any teenager should be able to tell you, was D.I.S.C.O.

I was about to be plunged back into pop purgatory, but this time I already had my lifejacket on.

I went in with eyes wide open knowing that what I was experiencing every Friday night was just something that had to be done.

♪ MY SUNDAY GIRL

I hung her

like a telephone

on my wall

she was atomic

and looked so fine

on plastic letters

I was in love

by parallel lines

and wished

I could have

met her

but she was in

another world

and i know

that we were

years apart

I waited for her

to call me

but I was only

dreaming

and when I woke

her picture

would fade away

shattering

my fragile heart

♪ ACROSS THE CROWDED DISCO ROOM

Life as a 6th former, in my last year of general education, was an idyllic existence, spoilt only by the occasional lesson and an overdose of Jeff Wayne. But it proved to be one of the most memorable periods of my teenage years

Having passed only four of the eight 'O' Levels I had sat back in Woking, it was deemed necessary to resit three of them at school in Germany. The main cause of this decision was my failure in Mathematics. Being one of the three 'R's I couldn't not finish my schooling without an acceptable grade, and this meant a C or above. The 'E' that I had received earlier would simply not do. So, my main focus was set on Maths, with Art and German as secondary subjects. With only three subjects in which to have lessons, I had a lot of free time which was spent in the 6th Form Common Room.

And it was quite a room. Comfy chairs around the walls, tables for resting your arms, or head on and a record player. The atmosphere was invariably nicotine flavoured smog and there was usually a minimum of three or four students there at any one time, actively being common. Of the three or four, two would always be Ozzie and Linda. No matter the day or the time, if you went to the common room, you could more or less guarantee that Ozzie and Linda would be there, in the corner, canoodling. I don't think they actually did any lessons. In fact, they seemed to be considerably older than the rest of us. I was only sixteen and not very mature in many ways, but those two seemed to be in their twenties at the least and in retrospect I suspect they were just hiding out, escapees from the reality of adult life. So, I just left them to it and got on with my strange new life of little lessons and copious commonness.

Meanwhile, back at the homestead in *am Osthoff* in Dülmen, social life was looking up. The gods had looked down and taken pity on me.

Back in Guildford I had gone to an all-boys school and had lived in a secluded cul-de-sac, away from the maddening crowd, where there were only seven other families in residence. I obviously knew what a girl was, I just didn't actually realise how many there were. Until I got to Germany. Now I was surrounded by them almost to the extent I couldn't go anywhere without bumping into one or more of them. They were everywhere, from living next door and across the road to round the corner and down the street. Hells belles, my sister even brought them home! And, to top it all, every Friday night, we were herded onto base to attend the weekly Youth Club D.I.S.C.O. where I could dance with them. The gods were indeed smiling at me.

Although I think I heard the occasional snicker as well because, as the old adage about horses and water springs to mind, I still didn't really have a clue what to do with them!

The weekly disco was, without a doubt, the most fun we had all week. It was a proper disco set up, coloured flashing lights, strobe, swirling bubble effect on the ceiling and walls, huge speakers and all topped off with a twin deck record layer with a slider button for fading one song out and another in whilst talking over it with a microphone. But the best part was that it was left to us, the youths, to operate it all and to keep the place rocking and jiving. Which we did quite admirably. The Club possessed its own collection of 7" singles of which there were ample to choose from. Barry, the YC leader (and father of the girl next door) used to grab every single in the top 40 whenever he went back to the UK on leave. So, while our play list was finite, it was certainly extensive.

I've had to resort to asking for help with remembering some of the catalogue. Still being in touch with several friends from that time helps and they have come up with many songs that I'd forgotten. What follows is a small cross section of the music that was popular at the top of the Seventies. This is what we bored teenagers gyrated and smooched and rocked and rolled and jived and boogied and danced and bumped and grinded to. Amy Stewart *'Knock On Wood,'* Bee Gees *'Stayin' Alive,'* Chic *'Le Freak,'* Edwin Starr *'Contact,'* Gloria Gaynor *'I Will Survive,'* M *'Pop Muzik,'* Donna Summer *'Hot Stuff,'*

Patrick Hernandez *'Born To Be Alive,'* Anita Ward *'Ring My Bell,'* City Boy *'5-7-0-5,'* Dan Hartman *'Instant Replay,'* Boney M. *'Rivers of Babylon/Brown Girl In The Ring,'* Kenny *'The Bump,'* Village People *'YMCA'* and *'In The Navy,'* Songs from Grease, Golden Earring *'Radar Love,'* and of course, a multitude of Status Quo songs. The list goes on and on for many more, too many for here, but thanks to Paul, Donna, Pam, Jo and Barry for your memories.

The Youth Club was obviously not the be all and end all of our disco experiences. There were other venues, other opportunities. One daring alternative for those old enough was the German disco in town. After much brain racking it's been decided it was called the Tenne, pronounced 'tenner'. This was a place where trouble could find you and where many of us 'youths' rarely went.

What the YC did was to instil in us all an inherent urge to dance and have fun. The urge certainly never left me. I'll get up and boogie to anything these days...I've always had the rhythm and I'll never lose it. And if I keep telling myself that, then I'll eventually believe it, just like everyone else.

The late Seventies produced so much good music that was enjoyable disco-dancing sounds back then, but still invokes involuntary foot-tapping and muscle-twitching today.

♪ You Wanted The Best And You Got It

Of course, whilst all this boogieing went on every Friday, we still had a week of school to get through beforehand, and at school I was able to make more friends that I would only ever see at school.

Due to the nature of the British Army On the Rhine (BAOR), their military presence was spread throughout Germany so the schools had quite large catchment areas with the pupils being bussed in from miles around. Our particular journey was around thirty miles and easily added a couple of hours onto each day. It was therefore possible to live anywhere from five or ten miles up to anything like eighty to a hundred miles away from some of your mates and school really was the only place you ever got to see them, unless there was the occasional Youth Club exchange visit.

One exception to this rule was my friend Kev. Actual name Kevan, not Kevin, but preferred Kev.

Kev lived in Münster itself and he is responsible for three quite significant things in the year I was at school with him.

First and foremost, and most heinous, it is he who shall be ever cursed for bringing Jeff Wayne's *War Of The Worlds* into the common room.

I think he possibly owned the record player too, which is probably why changing the record was a bit taboo, but for some reason whoever was in the room would always put that record on. Over and over. I can hear it now, in my mind. It drove me insane then and still does now. I mean, the chances of memories coming from then are a million to one, but still they come! Although, deep down, I grudgingly accept the musical genius of the album, I just refuse to own it.

Kev's second contribution to my musical enlightenment was to let me co-DJ with him. He had some actual disco equipment, decks, lights, mics, speakers etc, plus an admirable collection of records. It wasn't a huge set up but there was enough to put on a presentable show. We even cultivated an image to go with it. Based very loosely around the characters from A Clockwork Orange we would dress in white jeans, black shirts, braces, Doc Martens and a red bowler hat. We named this exciting new trendy style, Tryndale. Sadly, we seemed to be the only two dedicated followers of this fashion.

At one particular event, a wedding reception for one of the junior ranks, things were going well. One of the guests was extremely inebriated and was staggering all over the dance floor. Sensing it was time for a breather, Kev spoke the immortal line, *We'll buy a drink for anyone that dances to this.* As the track faded in, the dance area cleared in seconds, except for the drunk who stumbled around the deserted floor, dancing with his pint and spilling it everywhere. It was the first time I heard this song and it will always remain synonymous with that precise moment.

The song was *'Easy Livin'* by Uriah Heep and unless you know it, you need to listen to it to appreciate how fast it is. Needless to say, Kev dutifully bought the guy a pint who then quietly passed out a short while later, and the disco boogied on.

The Toc-H van used to come to *am Osthoff* every Sunday afternoon. Toc-H is a charitable organisation with soldiers' recreation and welfare at heart.

One of the services they used to provide was a mobile shop that sold all things imaginable from inside the back of a large van. It used to do its rounds every weekend, visiting all the military housing estates in a large area. As it happened, Kev was the assistant on the van that came our way. Too young to actually drive, this was his weekend job, the wages a handy supplement to fulfil his DJ aspirations

One Sunday the van turned up as usual. In no rush and in no need of anything from it I just sauntered toward it to chat with Kev as he stepped from the cab. But he rushed past me into the back of the van and quickly back out of it again before the driver/shopkeeper had even got to the back from the other side. Here, have this. You should listen to it. He thrust a shiny silver square thing at me and disappeared back into the van to carry out his duties, leaving me perplexed in the middle of the street, clutching ill-gotten gains.

Kev had just introduced me to the hottest band in the world. I was holding *Double Platinum,* the first Greatest Hits compilation by a strange looking group called KISS. And like the junkie after getting his first fix for free, I was hooked. The following week when the van came again, perhaps with a modicum of guilt, I legally bought Alive II (much better than Alive! apparently). And in the following months I added more KISS to my collection whenever funds could cover it. Albums such as *Destroyer, Hotter Than Hell, Love Gun, Dressed To Kill, Alive!* (eventually!), Kiss, and even *Dynasty* all became much treasured pieces of my ever growing collection.

I became a confirmed KISS freak. My most cherished purchase, from a record store in Dülmen town, were the solo albums that each of the band members produced in

1978. What made these extra special was that I had managed to acquire the picture disc version of each one. Gene, Ace, Peter and Paul in all their makeup and glorious technicolour etched into black vinyl. That set of four albums are one of the most prized possessions I ever owned.

My utter appreciation of Kiss was fairly short lived in the greater schism of things. 1979 until sometime around '81/82. I had just discovered (been introduced to) them too late in their career. In 1980 they released *Unmasked* and it was all over from there on in but that period of three or four years contained an incredible amount of likeability for their music.

My adulatory fandom culminated in a fancy dress competition at Hamm Youth Club (one of the aforementioned YC exchange visits). Four of us went dressed as members of KISS, me as Peter Criss. The reactions we received were incredible and the whole night was absolutely amazing.

Unfortunately, there were not enough prizes to go around and it had been decided to have a best Boy and best Girl prize. Whilst our costumes were without a doubt the best, we were not allowed to walk away with it. Luckily, with a very artistic piece of chest makeup, my sister Jo, dressed as Paul Stanley, won the best Girl costume but it was on behalf of the whole group. Best Boy went to some mummy dude wrapped in bandages for Christ's sake! But what a night it was. We were superstars for the night.

And all thanks to my mate Kev.

♪ BILL, CAROLINE, JOHNNY, RICK, FRANCIS, ALAN, JOHN AND ME

The end of the Seventies signified much more than just the end of a decade.

For me it was a turning point, not only of my adulthood, for I turned 18 in 1980, but also of my musical bias and my humour threshold. And much of this, well the music and the humour at least, was down to one man, dear old Bill Johnson.

Bill was one of a kind. He was a soldier, with a family, and lived somewhere in Dülmen alongside the rest of us.
He was also one of a special group of people that gave up their spare time, for free, to help out with the various activities laid on by the Youth Club. Although with Bill, and I may be wrong but it's just the impression I got, he went one step further with these particular occasions and actually organized everything.

February 6th 1979 is/was an auspicious date in my life. You, the avid reader, will have already learnt of my growing appreciation of all things Quoesque. Well this date would prove to be the zenith of my awakening, from which I would emerge as a full blown, head-banging, mind-numbing, foot-stomping, 12 bar boogie boy, no nonsense, denim-clad, Quo fan for life.

It was just another of those occasions that you take for granted when you're young. It didn't matter who organized it, who the bus driver was, who had to give up spare time, what the actual cost was (apart from our tickets) and so forth, it just didn't matter. We were going to the Hälle Münsterland, to see the mighty Quo! T-shirts, Doc Martens and denim were in abundance, as was long hair. There was a lot of English youth there that had travelled in from all over the area like we had, but I think there were probably more Germans there, though strangely enough, it was hard to tell the difference.

At my first gig, the wonderful ELO at Wembley Arena the previous year, we had been guided towards row upon row of plastic seating, where audience participation had been limited to stand up or sit down.

Hälle Münsterland was a whole new wonderful ballgame. And the whole idea of the game was to get as upfront and personal as you could because the closer you were to the front, the more pleasurable the experience would be.

By the time the gig blasted off I was closer to a Fräulein than I would ever be. I never did get to see her face, but she had the softest arse I've ever been crammed up against. Her boyfriend however had terrible BO, and I can't say I was sorry when the natural swell of the crowd separated us forever. But I was still up near the front, hemmed in by a faceless denim mob, baying for their heroes.

An easy cliché to use would be to say that I caught Status Quo at their peak but, when you look back over their incredible career it would be hard to say exactly when they did reach it, although those halcyon years would be a close runner for the title.

I was lucky enough to see the 'original' line up, the Frantic Four, long hair and all, of, Rick Parfitt, Francis Rossi, Alan Lancaster and John Coghlan.

A bit of research has shown that the gig kicked off with *'Caroline'* swiftly followed by *'Rollover Lay Down'* and then *'Backwater.'* To say I was mesmerized would be an understatement. This truly was what I was born to do. It wasn't adulation, idolatry or even unctuous worship... it was just goddam fucking awesome and I lost myself to the noise of the atmosphere, the beat and the rhythm, the adrenalin of the applause, the proximity of heat and the gasp of cool air as you stretched your neck upwards, the luxury of a split second of space to move as the crowd surged, the cocktail of mingling odours and the fantastic visions of the light displays. And. The. Music.

This was also about the time that Rick Parfitt possibly recognized me from a previous existence. As is the norm with rock gigs then, and these days, the band usually explode into action with a blistering entrance of noise and light and let rip for two or three songs. Then they catch their breath and say hello to the crowd and engage in a little banter etc. Francis Rossi of the Quo was a master of this and would usually start this session off with a loud 'Ello! This would result in numerous responses from the crowd to which he and the band would reply with various gestures or spoken words of greeting or recognition. This night was no exception. After the third or fourth song they had a breather and Francis did his thing and the crowd did theirs. Just as everything was settling back down in readiness for the next song that Francis was introducing, I leapt upwards as high as I could and shouted at the top of my voice Hello! just as Rick Parfitt happened to be looking in my general direction as he surveyed the crowd of expectant faces. He acknowledged my upward appearance and exclaimed 'Ello! And I haven't washed since.

The thing about Quo, 'though was their unerring commitment to touring and putting on shows for their fans, Admittedly their tours always seemed to coincide with yet another album release, such is the way of the music hype market, but back in those days things weren't much different

The show in Münster was but just one date on their European *'If You Can't Stand The Heat'* tour to promote the 1978 album of the same name. This was a pretty lacklustre album, let down in the first instance by its unimaginative cover and then more so by the songs on it. Perhaps they felt this way about the album too, deep down, for they only played three songs from it at various points in the play list. Namely, *Gonna Teach You To Love Me, Like a Good Girl,* and *Oh! What A Night.* The rest of the list was comprised of the old skool favourites that still set the house alight today... *Rain, Roadhouse Blues, Big Fat Mama, 4500 Times, Down Down* and the inevitable ultimate encore farewell, *Bye Bye Johnny.*

This was the Quo that I would love from that day forth.

I'd go to see them Again and Again, 'cos The Party Ain't Over Yet.

♪ RICK SAYS HELLO

Take me back to daze

of denim and twelve

bar powerchord

boogie

when riffs

let rip from a

Marshall mountain

and we breathed in purple

haze

show me again

the magnificent tits

of girls above the crowd

and let me chant

the name of the band

that played their music

loud

we packed in tight

a heaving sea

of patchouli leather

and flailing hair

and as our fists

punched the

night

rick hushed his tele

and said hello

to me

♪ RICHIE? OH YEAH! GRAHAM BONNET? INCREDIBLE VOCALIST!

If you were asked to name something memorable from your youth, an activity or occurrence as opposed to a specific object, person or event, I wonder how many would eventually come up with going to the cinema?

The weekly Saturday morning matinee when you were real young, when you would burst out of the exit after the show and be blinded by the bright daylight and then re-enact the roles of the heroes and villains you'd just been cheering or booing, all the way home.

Or maybe when you were a bit older, and you got to go to the Saturday or Sunday afternoon showings of movies more suited to your age than the kiddie's matinees.

And then, older still, you would maybe go out on a Friday or Saturday evening to see the latest blockbuster. If you were really lucky you might take a girl and even get to sit in the extra wide double seats in the back row.

Such was life before VCR's, DVD's, SKY Box Office, LED TV's and PC's with their streaming videos and bit torrents off the interweb.

The cinema was about as technological as it got and gave great entertainment.

Unless of course you were an army kid, living in Dülmen, in Germany.

We had three choices. Well, four if you count 'do nothing.'

One, visit the 'cinema' room on base. This was a room with rows of chairs, not seating mind but plastic stackable chairs, and a projector screen. They would occasionally play a movie on one of those big reel to reel movie projector things that flickered a lot and made a flapping noise as though it was about to take off.

They had the audacity to refuse me entry to watch Saturday Night Fever once, because I wasn't 18.

Apparently, it didn't make any difference when I pointed out that they weren't actually a cinema, although with hindsight it probably made it worse. But that was the first and only time I was ever refused entry because of my age.

Two, visit the German cinema in town. Which, unless you spoke fluent German, was a waste of time because they dubbed every film with German voiceovers. The only time we ever went there was when *Grease* first came out. A whole bunch of us were very keen to see it and decided that the songs were the most important part so we would go and watch it anyway because it would likely be ages before we got the chance to see the proper English version. It was kind of strange seeing John Travolta and Olivia Newton-John speaking badly synched German but singing in perfect English. But we were happy. We had seen the movie.

And three...visit the English run cinema, showing English speaking films and full of English audiences. The only drawback was that it was, like most other stuff, in

Münster, and therefore not a viable option. I only ever went once.

And that 'once' was courtesy of none other than dear old Bill Johnson who, a few months earlier, took a load of us to see the mighty Quo. I'm sure I'm not the only one that holds Bills memory in such high esteem. He truly was a likeable and affable guy with a wickedly dry sense of humour. He had one of those faces too, that could just pull an expression at which you could not fail to laugh. We used to laugh a lot when he was around, which made his choice of film all the more understandable.

Sometime in either late 1979 or early 1980, Bill organized an outing for a small group of reprobates to the cinema in Münster to see *'The Life Of Brian'* and my love affair with Monty Python was both instigated and consummated in one foul thrust.

Laugh? I almost wet myself. Up until that point in my life it was the funniest thing I had ever seen or heard, and I spent many magical moments in the ensuing years reliving it through countless re-runs of first, the VHS recordings, and then the DVD, though I don't think I ever got the Blu-ray version.

I also adopted the end-scene song *'Always Look On The Bright Side Of Life'* as my signature tune and had, and still have, at least two t-shirts featuring those very words.

But from that day, I was a confirmed Python fan, and I went on to truly appreciate their very special and unique brand of humour and, not least of all, their brilliant musical offerings.

I hate buying compilation albums with a passion but *'Monty Python Sings'* is an excellent accompaniment to any true aficionados' collection, featuring many of their best-known numbers from their catalogue of films such as *The Meaning of Life* and *The Holy Grail,* and also previous albums.

A few years later, when I sold off my vast vinyl collection, the only records I didn't get rid of, apart from my 12" picture disc single of *'Freebird'* and the *Diamond Head* white label EP featuring *'Shoot Out The Lights'* and, *'Am I Evil'* bought at their gig, was my Monty Python collection. And I still have them all these years later.

Bill Johnson, RIP...thank you for awaking my humour.

But Bill's influence on my awakening was not quite over. Just over a year after the magnificent and mighty Quo, we were once more in his company and on our way to the Hälle Münsterland again. This time it was to see a band featuring the guitarist from Deep Purple that had captured my imagination in Brussels when I bought their Stormbringer album. Richie Blackmore, one of THE ultimate guitar playing demigods that ever lived, actually left Deep Purple not long after that much maligned album and formed the much marvelled Richie Blackmore's Rainbow, or just Rainbow. In February 1980 the line-up consisted of Blackmore on guitar, Cozy Powell on drums, Roger Glover as bassist, Don Airey on keyboards and the awesome Graham Bonnet as frontman with the mic.

Although Ronnie James Dio, whom Bonnet replaced, would go on to greater things as a soloist I regret never having witnessed his participation in Rainbow.

We caught Rainbow during their *Down To Earth* promo tour. It's a known fact that no two Rainbow albums feature the same line-up. The only constant being Richie Blackmore himself. A bit like the modern-day Guns 'n' Roses and Axl Rose really. But like their modern-day counterparts, their disjointed origins still managed to produce music of awesome proportions.

The only three songs of any note that spring to mind from the album are *'Since You've Been Gone,' 'Lost In Hollywood,'* and *'All Night Long'.* All these were played at the gig as was, I'm sure, *'Love's No Friend'* and *'Makin' Love.'* But as with most all Rainbow gigs, it opened with the immortal lines from the Wizard of Oz movie...oh come on... you know the line, don't make me say it... let me just say Mr. Bonnet let rip with *'Somewhere Over The Rainbow,'* after which we were treated to renditions of the likes of *'Kill The King,' 'Man*

On The Silver Mountain,' 'Stargazer,' 'Catch The Rainbow' and *'Long Live Rock N Roll.'*

Graham Bonnet was powerfully awesome to the extreme and Richie Blackmore was just a demigod. I recall standing spellbound as he played a solo, in darkness except for a single spotlight shining down on him, on which he used his highly polished Stratocaster to reflect the light around the audience. Someone in the crowd got impatient and threw a bottle at him which actually bounced off the guitar.

The demigod didn't even flinch, although if looks could kill, he would have been still languishing in a German prison, but he sure as hell reflected those beams right back at the bottle throwing perp like he was Luke Skywalker having a barney with his dad.

The Rainbow gig was not as energetic as the Quo spectacular, but it was far more immersive and went an awful long way toward my appreciation of epic rock tunes. I can still, almost word perfect, sing Stargazer at full blast and literally enjoy doing it. Next step is to sing it while playing it on my guitar.

Rainbow. I loved you then and love you still.

♪ ABOUT FAST FOOD, LOVE, LIFE, AND DEATH

1980 was probably the most defining year of my youth.

If my 18th birthday, in the June of that year, was to be my passing from adolescent to adult, then the previous two years had been, as well as formative, my *Rites of Passage.*

I had sat my exams again, fallen in and out of love several times, left school, started work, popped my cherry, seen Monty Python, attended a proper party, watched porn, been a DJ, publicly confirmed my metal head status, got totally legless, gone to two major gigs and participated in a search party for a missing six year old girl, amongst other things.

It was certainly an eventful couple of years.

I had indeed passed my exams this time round, albeit with the barest minimum grades, C's throughout in Maths, German and Art.

I actually left school on my 17th birthday, the one and only day I ever got drunk at school. I sneaked in a bottle of Apfelschnapps and surreptitiously sipped it all day. In hindsight, I think I am actually still at school because I don't really recall coming home that day.

Although it was my birthday, getting drunk wasn't really the most sensible of things to do considering that I started work the next day.

Discounting my first job, a Saturday job at a Christian bookshop in Guildford, work was a wonderful new experience for me.

I was graded as a C3 Civilian and worked for the Army on the base in Dülmen. I was the Rations Storeman, keeping stock of all the foodstuffs required by the various Messes and the Nursery School, according to what was ordered. I would travel three times a week in a Bedford TK truck, with a German driver, to Münster to collect the rations, distributing the fresh stuff on the way back and putting the dry goods into stock in MY storeroom.

By day, my storeroom was a great place to be. No stress, unlike the jobs of modern-day life... well, except when Captain Westbrook, the Quartermaster, did his weekly stock check, but even that usually went off without a hitch. Free food was also in abundance, courtesy of the jolly and rotund cooks of the Catering Corps. I earned money for counting food and life was good. I got to spend the wages whenever I wanted, and on whatever I wanted. Usually, I spent around half of it on drink, food, girlfriends and general good times and then just wasted the rest. But at the age of seventeen, no transport and in a foreign country, there are limits to what is actually achievable in the pursuit of hedonism. Mostly we found ourselves in the local bar for drink and the *schnellie* for food.

Schnell Imbiss - Fast service, referring to a fast food snack bar. Sort of an early German forerunner to McDonalds but much nicer. What I wouldn't give right now for a Bratty or a Fricky!

During my time in Germany, although I do not recall exactly when it was, I had my first experience of meeting someone from my past. I never knew his name the first-time round, because when you are ten you just don't ask guitar playing demigods what their name is. I've been racking my brains to remember his name from then and also from this time in Germany but to no avail, so I shall just refer to him as Chris.

This time around, Chris was no longer a gangly guitar-playing teenager but a fully-fledged soldier, complete with German wife and a very cute six-year-old daughter. I did not have much to do with him but vividly recall the moment that the memory of him surfaced, when I asked him if he had ever been to Belgium and his resultant questions as to how I knew that. When I indicated his deformed finger and how I remembered his guitar playing in a Belgian forest, our acquaintance was acknowledged.

One night, sometime in early 1980, a bunch of us decided to go to the schnellie for some quick food and a few beers. When we came out, we came out to general uproar in the English-speaking quarters. Heidi, the adorable six-year-old daughter of Chris and his German wife, had gone missing earlier in the evening and simply everyone was getting ready to search for her. Needless to say, we all made ourselves available and soon there were groups heading out in all directions with torches and whistles to search the surrounding areas. The local nursery school in *Am Osthoff Strasse* was seconded as the central coordination point and my CB radio was set up to keep in contact with those in cars equipped with CB too. The search went on long into the night with probably around two to three hundred people involved.

But there was no sign or trace. The decision was made by the local authority late on in the night to drain the lake. With search all but called off, many involved had nothing more to do but await the result of the lake draining

It was probably around 2am when the level dropped low enough for them to see her body. No foul play was suspected but a huge pall of sadness descended. Heidi was a well-known little individual, happy and bi-lingual; she had made an impression on many people, not least some of my group of friends who had been her baby-sitter on occasion. And now she was gone... her last moments a horrific mystery.

There was no music that night, or for a few nights after. There was much self-recrimination for we had encountered Heidi, playing in the street, on our way to the schnellie. And if I had a time machine, that single moment would be uppermost on my list of destinations.

I didn't have much more interaction with Chris after that. The community was in shock for several weeks and time just sort of whittled away until our departure from Germany in the June.

♪ HELLO!

In February 1979, at the Hälle Munsterland in Germany, I watched with envy as some kid caught John Cohglan's drumstick when he threw it into the crowd after a pretty awesome solo.

A little later I felt the greenness returning when Francis Rossi, once he had finished mopping his glistening brow, hurled his sweat-soaked towel into the assembled mass of an adoring audience. A brief melee ensued until I saw it held triumphantly aloft like a trophy or the spoils of war. I could only curse myself for having chosen to stand here, instead of over there in the direct line of fire.

I had the last laugh though, for during a lull in the lively proceedings and once the band finished trading greetings and jocularities with the audience, I waited until the absolute last moment. Then, just as I sensed that they were about to start the next number, I jumped as high as I could and shouted out

"Hello!"

Rick Parfitt happened to be looking in my direction and he shouted back, to me, "'Ello!"

The rest of the gig was a blur. I didn't get a drumstick or a smelly towel. I maintain that with Mr. Parfitt's personal greeting I got something far better. Nothing tangible, but something that will always be with me. The drumstick would have been nice though.

A year later I was back in the UK, my brat-pack travels as a dependent of the British Army well and truly behind me. As a newly turned 18-year-old my adult life was just starting, and what better way to kick it off than a two-hundred-mile trip to Leeds to meet a friend, then another one fifty or so to Stafford to see the Hottest Band In The World.

My love of KISS, courtesy of my mate Kev in Germany, has been well documented. The fact I was now making this pilgrimage to see them play, here in the UK for the first time, was testament to my adulation.

September the 5th, 1980. A date that is synonymous with my musical enlightenment. Only my fourth ever gig but by far the most important to me. It was symbolic of a Rite of Passage. It would be the furthest I travelled on my own to an event I had wholly planned, organised and paid for myself.

The buzz in Stafford was incredible. Special buses had been laid on from the train station to Bingley Hall. The venue was a heaving sea of denim, hair and leather, and it was packed solid. Arriving quite late we agreed there was no way of working our way toward the front of the crowd, so we stood our ground toward the back and waited for the show to start.

Researching that show now and thinking back to then, I don't think I was aware at the time, but the tour was called the *'Unmasked'* tour which was also the name of their latest album. Yes, that album. If *Dynasty* had marked the beginning of the end, then *Unmasked* merely proved the cynics right.

Also unbeknown to me at the time was that this tour was to be the last that featured Ace Frehely (well, for 16 years anyway). One sad fact that I was aware of though, was that this would be the first tour that did not feature the percussionist talents of Peter Criss, having left to be replaced by Eric Carr.

But all of that didn't really matter. I got totally blown away by the show. I saw Gene Simmons fly across the heads of the crowd, spewing forth blood as it erupted from his mouth. I saw fireworks and flames and incredible lighting. I saw Space Ace let go of his guitar which then rose into the air, smoking and sparking until he went off stage and came back with another one. He then proceeded to shoot pulses of light at the floating guitar until it exploded in flames and fell to the floor whereupon he smashed it into pieces and showered them onto the crowd. Marooned at the back, not even close enough to have been slightly spattered by Gene's bloody spittle, I could only feel rising morosity as another missed opportunity to catch a piece of rock memorabilia passed me by.

I made do with a silk scarf and a program, and an early morning ride on the milk train back to Leeds. But at least KISS was crossed off the list and I had another memory that would never be forgotten, even if the 'Catch Something Thrown By A Rockstar' tick box still remained elusively blank.

As the Eighties finally escaped from the shadow of the Seventies, the most notable thing happening on the music scene was the New Wave absurdity, which was all hairdos, make-up, fashionable clothing and romanticism. And that was just the boys.

Our ears were assailed by the warblings of the likes of Soft Cell, Adam Ant, Boy George, Altered Images, The Human League, Duran Duran, Depeche Mode... the list is endless and I'm sure you get the picture. But once more, lines were being drawn in the sand, across which no true metal head would dare step.

Luckily for the denim mob, we had our own new wave going on. Back then it was just another new band, another great gig, another awesome album. As good as or better than the last, sometimes not, but in all cases, it was music being created.

These days, that era is reverently referred to as NWOBHM, pronounced NEWWOBBEM. Quite simply, we were living through the New Wave Of British Heavy Metal. One of the great exponents of the genre at the time was a radio 1 DJ by the name of Tommy Vance who hosted The Friday Night Rock Show on the radio.

And through the dark times of *'Tainted Love,'* *'Karma Chameleon,'* and *'Ant Music'* we sought solace and refuge by tuning in to 'TV on the Radio'.

And into this melting pot of musical mayhem came an urge within me to experience more and more live music. The closest and most convenient venue was the now sadly departed, West Runton Pavilion. A legendary and hallowed place in the annals of rock concert history. A place where up and coming bands, too numerous to mention, cut their teeth on the tour circuit. Tucked away far up on the

North Norfolk coast it was probably one of the most unlikely locations ever thought of, but it welcomed with open arms young bands such as Thin Lizzy, Black Sabbath, ACDC, Blue Oyster Cult, Status Quo and Iron Maiden to name but a few.

The biggest band I got to see there was the incredible Motorhead, on their Bomber tour. I was also lucky to see Magnum, Saxon and my piece de resistance, the wonderful Diamond Head.

They were a four man band from Stourbridge and their popularity soon earned them a cult following. By 1979 they were supporting big acts such as ACDC and Iron Maiden so by the time I saw them in '82 they were well established as a noted forerunner of the NWOBHM phenomena. Later in the Eighties they would be cited as a major influence by bands such as Metallica and Megadeth.

But I didn't really care about much of that. I was in seventh heaven. We had arrived in good time, fought a path to the bar and grabbed a four pack of the notorious Breakers Malt Liquor, the only known beer that could bang the inside of a headbangers head while he banged his head to headbanging music. It was a required source of sustenance while stuck in the middle of the heaving crowd. But I'd gone one better and actually made it to the front, for the first ever time. In the heady days of pre-Health and Safety officialdom there were no safety barriers to contend with. Being at the front meant leaning on the actual stage. West Runton Pavilion was my church, and I was at the altar. Finally.

The set list is lost to the ether. If you know anything about Diamond Head, you'd recognise the titles of the songs I know they played such as *'It's Electric,' 'Sucking My Love,' 'Shoot Out The Lights,' 'Helpless,'* and of course, the indomitable *'Am I Evil?'*

Much of what they played back then have gone on to become classic rock songs, and are often heard on rock radio stations today.

And there I was, in total awe of these guitar playing demigods (and the drummer of course) offering my soul in exchange for eternal rock 'n' fuckin' roll ecstasy.

And then it happened. Brian Tatler, founding member, lead guitarist and all-round, long-haired, nice guy, finished whichever song they had just been playing and threw his plectrum into the crowd. Or to be more precise, he threw it at me, and I caught the damn thing!

Words cannot adequately describe my feelings at that exact moment. My devotion to the faith had paid off and my reward was just and fitting.

It was no drumstick, or splinter of broken guitar.

It was a small triangular piece of black plastic with rounded points and embossed with the immortal words 'Gibson Medium' in silver.

And all these years later, I still have that particular piece of manna, along with the autographed program which I got them to sign when I went backstage after the gig and met them all, to shake their hands, and say

"Hello!"

♪ THE DENIM EMOTIVE

The aroma of patchouli

mingles with a waft

of marijuana enhancing

but not disguising

the overpowering

proximity of perspiring

people clad in denim

and leather

an electric ambiance

of anticipation

whips the crowd

into a premature

frenzy but there is

no submission

only impatience

the cacophony is

deafening as

we urge

we implore

we demand

our heroes to appear

with whistles and cheers

and chants of their name

and finally

there is darkness

the mood changes

to one of urgency

the crescendo toward

the long awaited orgasm

of aural satisfaction

begins with the throaty

deep throttle of a Harley

on heat

dazzling and furious

the stage erupts

in a glorious explosion

of white light as a

soundwave tsunami

is expelled from the

house-high stack of
amplifiers when the
first chord is struck

the crowd surges
in excitement as the
play list begins
and a few rows ahead
a girl sitting astride
the shoulders of her friend
exposes her magnificent
tits as a heartfelt
thank you to the band

deafened voiceless and spent
with our orgasm achieved
the end of the gig
always left me wanting more

with the passing of time
I shall always have these
memories of my love affair

with live music

all I can do now though

is pull on my jeans

and crank up the stereo

all that's missing

are the breasts

♪ OUTRO

And there you have it... seven short years in the life of a teenager. An awakening. A gradual realisation that there is a bigger meaning to everything. And then a total acceptance of, and immersion into, this wonderful new way of life.

The end of this era was marked by the Diamond Head gig around my twentieth birthday. Within the next two years I would be married and become a father to my firstborn, Kevin. My record collection would be sold off to pay for baby equipment and I certainly wouldn't be going to any more gigs.

Not for a few years anyway...

♪ ACKNOWLEDGEMENTS

To the fantabulous Mr. Meek without whom these memoirs might not have seen the light of day-

Thank you for your support and creative input.

Thanks also to Jo, Pam, Donna, Barry and Paul for bump-starting my memory.

And finally, a shout out to musicians everywhere...

Thank you for the music...

♪ AUTHOR

ANDY GREENHOUSE

♫ ABOUT THE AUTHOR

Andy Greenhouse should have been a musician but was last in the queue when they were handing out the ability to play a musical instrument, and even further back than the back in the 'Who wants to be a singer?' queue. So, he had to make do with just writing about it. And that is what he has done here with his first foray into stringing consecutive sentences together in the hope they make sense, to someone, anyone.

More at home with pushing his poetry onto his dear readers, having previously published a couple of collections this, almost auto-biographical, account of how music has affected and influenced his experience of life was borne of a desire to join the dots of the coincidences and connections that have followed his every step.

Born in the ancient Norfolk market town of Thetford, but carried, like the dandelion seed, to places all over the world to enjoy a richly varied and multi-cultured upbringing courtesy of his father's military postings. Music soon found him and, like a little lost puppy, started following him around and nipping at his aural senses for attention.

Nowadays his feet are firmly rooted back in his hometown and the only traveling is done when holidaying abroad. But he's at his happiest when going gigging or to a festival.

This book has been a work in progress for as long as he can remember, taking so long due to the music not stopping because, as we all know, stuff only happens between the music.

♪ PUBLISHER

INHERIT
THE EARTH
PUBLICATIONS.

ONLINE
PUBLISHERS.

inherit_theearth@btinternet.com

♪ NOTES

Printed by Amazon Italia Logistica S.r.l.
Torrazza Piemonte (TO), Italy